Our STATUE of LIBERTY

THELMA NASON

Illustrated by Adolph Le Moult

MODERN CURRICULUM PRESS

ISBN: 0-8136-5960-4
Printed in the United States of America

11 12 13 14 15   06

1-800-321-3106
www.pearsonlearning.com

The Statue of Liberty is one of America's greatest treasures. Thousands of people visit it every year. Most of them go up into the seven-pointed crown. From its many windows, they look across New York Harbor to the skyscrapers of the city. They learn that this is the biggest statue in the world. With its base, it is taller than a twenty-five story building.

Americans love Miss Liberty because everything about her shows our freedom. The book in her left hand carries the date of our nation's birth, July 4, 1776. The broken chain at her feet means that we became free by breaking away from England. The rays of her torch show how our liberty lights the way for the rest of the world.

All Americans today are proud of Miss Liberty. She was a gift to our country from the people of France.

Frédéric Auguste Bartholdi
1835-1904
DESIGNER AND SCULPTOR OF THE STATUE OF LIBERTY

Our STATUE of LIBERTY

Modern Curriculum Press
BEGINNING
TO
READ
Series

One night in 1865, some French writers, artists, and scholars were talking about America. They spoke of the history of the friendship between their country and ours. A young French nobleman, Lafayette, had gone to America in 1777. He helped the colonies, who were fighting for their freedom from England. He became like a son to George Washington. Later, he asked the French

government to help the colonies. The Americans loved Lafayette as they did their own heroes.

The men present that night spoke further of the tie between France and the United States.

One man said that if a monument to American independence were ever built in the United States, it should be built by both countries, since they had fought together for American independence.

Frédéric Bartholdi, a well-known French sculptor, was one of the group. He thought a monument to American independence would be fine. He began to work on plans for it. But war broke out in France, and he could not go on with his exciting plans.

Six years later, the same group of men gathered for dinner. Once again the talk was of America.

Bartholdi spoke of the coming celebration in the United States of the one hundredth birthday of their independence. He thought of making a great statue for this occasion.

His friends agreed. They thought that it should be given by the people of France to the people of America as a sign of friendship. They asked Bartholdi to visit America and choose a place for it.

So Bartholdi set out for the United States in 1871. He hoped to have drawings for his idea finished when he landed, but none that he did on board ship satisfied him.

When he reached New York Harbor, he stared with surprise at the wide bay and the city beyond. How large it was and how beautiful! As the ship passed a small island,

Bedloe's Island, he suddenly knew that this was the place for his statue. And he knew exactly how he wanted it to look.

It would be a woman holding a torch above her head. She must be very large to match the great bay. Her torch would light the way for ships, as American freedom lighted the world. The artist drew a picture of his idea.

Bartholdi met President Grant and other important Americans while he was in the United States. He showed them his pictures and explained his plan. These people were very interested. They thought America should build a base for the statue.

When Bartholdi returned to France, he
made a small model of the statue. His friends
were very pleased with it. He went on with his
work while they started to collect money to
build the statue. Grown-ups and children all
over France gave to show their friendship
for America.

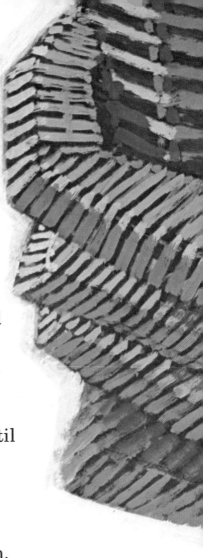

The United States was
planning a big fair in 1876
to celebrate its one hundredth
birthday. It was not possible
for Bartholdi to finish the
entire statue by that time.
So he decided to send the
hand and torch alone.

He and his helpers worked
for long hours. They built a
huge wood and plaster mold of
the hand and torch. They
hammered sheets of copper until
they fitted the mold exactly.
These copper sheets were
fastened together and held in
place by rods and bands of iron.
This was the way the entire
statue would be built.

At the fair in Philadelphia, visitors crowded around the great hand holding the torch. They stared at the index finger, which was eight feet long.

In New York, people worked together
to raise money for the base of the statue.
They worked hard to get rich men to give
large sums. The base was started on Bedloe's
Island in 1883. But it soon became clear
that there was not enough money to finish the
job. Many people from the West still did not
understand what the statue was for. They
thought the torch would be only a lighthouse
for New York.

In Bartholdi's big workshop, the copper sheets
were beaten into shape. When they were
finished, they were carried into the courtyard.
Here they were put into place on a high steel
frame.

Early in 1884, Miss Liberty was finished.
Rising from the courtyard, she looked out
over the rooftops of Paris. People looked at
her with awe. She was huge, but perfect. They
marvelled at her mouth, which was a yard
wide, and at her eyes, which were each more
than two feet across.

On July 4, 1884, Miss Liberty became an American. She was given to the United States in an official ceremony, though she would stay in Paris until her base was ready. Bartholdi hoped that this work would be done more quickly, now that the Americans owned the statue. But it did not work out that way.
The money that had been collected was almost gone. Nobody was giving any more.

Months passed and finally Bartholdi decided it was time to ship the statue to America. It would take months to take the statue apart, crate it, and ship it. He thought the base would surely be finished by that time.

But only a few feet of Miss Liberty's base had been built. Work had completely stopped because there was no more money. The people who were collecting it had forgotten that in a democracy everyone is important. They did not ask all the people to help.

Fortunately one American realized this and cared enough to fight for more money for the base. His name was Joseph Pulitzer. He owned an important newspaper, the New York *World*, which he called "the people's paper." He believed that the American

people would pay for the base if they had the chance. He wrote an article reminding people that the statue had been built with money given by many people all over France. "Give something," he wrote, "however little. . . ."

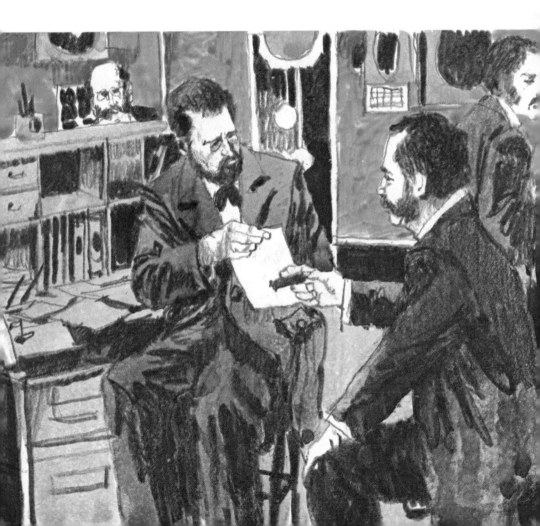

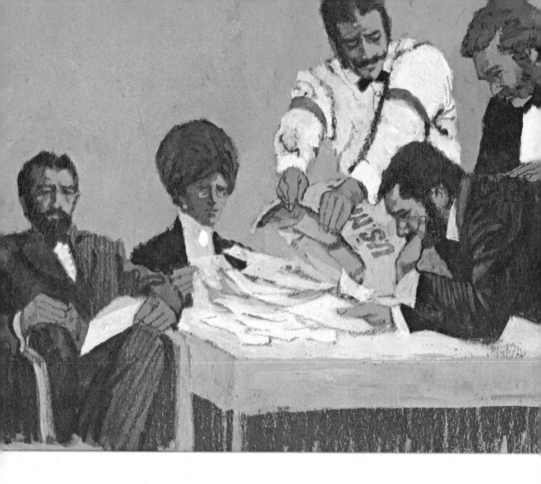

The people answered Mr. Pulitzer just as
he thought they would. Money began coming
in from all parts of the country. People sent
what they could, even if it was no more than
fifty cents. School children sent their nickels
and dimes. To show that every person was

important, the *World* published the name of everyone who gave, no matter what the amount. Only 147 days after Mr. Pulitzer's article appeared, the *World* proudly published the news that there was enough money to finish the base.

October 28, 1886, was a great day in New York. It was the day set for unveiling the statue. Workmen had been busy for months fastening the copper sheets to the frame on Bedloe's Island. Bartholdi himself had come at the beginning to discuss the plans with the builder. Miss Liberty was now ready. She stood proudly on her base built by American men and women, boys and girls. Her face was covered with the flag of France.

The day was cold and rainy, but nothing could stop the celebration. A parade that lasted over three hours marched down Broadway. The main part of the program was held on the island. A platform had been built at the feet of the statue. On it sat the American President with important men from both France and the United States. Far above, Bartholdi waited in the head of the statue. He was to have the honor of pulling the rope that would drop the flag from Miss Liberty's face.

From his high place, Bartholdi could see nothing but fog beneath him. But he knew that the harbor was crowded with boats of all kinds. Thousands of people on those boats were waiting to see the face of the statue.

Bartholdi heard cheering from the platform and saw the signal for the unveiling. He pulled the rope.

A great noise rose from the harbor. Bells clanged. Firecrackers popped. Tugboats hooted, and whistles screamed.

Above the noise, the statue seemed to smile as she held her torch. The people of a great democracy were welcoming her. Miss Liberty had found her home.

In 1982, workers discovered that Miss Liberty was beginning to show signs of her age. Acid rain had worn thin her copper covering. Parts of her right arm and the torch that it holds had fallen into New York Harbor.

When President Reagan heard the alarming news, he organized a federal commission to help raise funds to repair the Statue of Liberty in time for its 100th birthday. President Reagan knew that ordinary people from the United States and France had paid for the building of the statue. He felt that the people of America would be happy to share the cost of getting it repaired. And he was right! Children and adults from all over the United States gave whatever they could to mend Miss Liberty.

The Statue of Liberty is respected all over the world. Thanks to the care and love of the American people, it will continue to hold out the promise of freedom for many years to come.